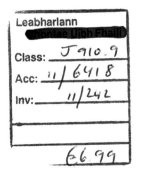

What I Like
The Seaside

Liz Lennon

W
FRANKLIN WATTS
LONDON•SYDNEY

Today, we are off to the seaside.

I hope I see the sea first!

The seaside is my favourite place.

I love the sound of the **waves.**

Phew! Today it's hot. My hat keeps me cool.

Dad rubs in sun cream
so I don't burn.

Fill up
the bucket.
Pat it with
a spade.

Making sandcastles is fun. Do you like mine?

Look how far
I can kick
a ball.

Dad wants a rest.

I want to play all day.

Splash! It's time to cool off in the water. I love paddling.

Look, some little fish are swimming.

What other animals can I find? Noisy seagulls are easy to spot.

A rock pool is full of animals.
Look at the crab walking sideways!

I'm hungry. It's time for a picnic.

Oh no, some sand got into this sandwich!

I like to eat ice cream on the beach.

I have to eat quickly.

My ice cream is melting in the sun.

I like collecting seashells.
Some feel smooth
and some
are rough.

Shells with swirly patterns are my favourite. Can you see one?

Look, the sea is washing away my sandcastle.

It's time to go home. I can still hear the sound of the sea in my shell!

About this book

The seaside is a place most children enjoy spending time and there are plenty of opportunities for learning. Looking at and talking about the pictures in this book is a good starting point. Here are some ideas for further talking points:

Travelling What ways would they like to go to the seaside - by car, train or would they like to fly abroad?

Favourite things What is their favourite thing to do at the seaside? Collecting seashells, playing games, swimming, making sandcastles? How do you make a sandcastle?

Keeping safe Why do we need to be careful of the sun when we spend all day outside? How can we keep safe? (Sun cream and covering up.) You could also discuss staying with parents or carers at the seaside - the sea can be dangerous and they should be near their carers at all times.

Wildlife There are plenty of plants and animals to talk about including seaweed (how does it feel?), rock-pool wildlife, fish and seaside birds.

Seaside foods Ice cream is an obvious favourite. What do they like about it? Which is their favourite flavour? What other seaside foods do they like: candyfloss, fish and chips, picnics etc?

First published in 2011 by Franklin Watts

Copyright © Franklin Watts 2011

Franklin Watts
338 Euston Road
London NW1 3BH

Franklin Watts Australia
Level 17/207 Kent Street
Sydney, NSW 2000

All rights reserved.

Printed in China

Dewey number: 910.9'146
ISBN: 978 1 4451 0467 6

Series Editor: Sarah Peutrill
Art Director: Jonathan Hair
Series Designer: Paul Cherrill
Picture Researcher: Diana Morris
Consultants: Karina Philip and Deborah Cox

Franklin Watts is a division of Hachette Children's Books, an Hachette UK company.

www.hachette.co.uk

Picture credits: Alamy: Petr Bonek 8; Allen Brown 18; P.Broze & A. Chederros 2; SPL 7. Ecoscene: Chinch Gryniewicz 15. Istockphoto: Demid Borodin 22; Alain Cassiede 17; Maria Pavlova 1, 9; K Zenouli 3. Shutterstock: Andi Berger 20; Dimos 13; Dana E Fry 11;Daniel Gale 4; Warren Goldswain 10; Rob Marmion front cover; Tomasz Niewieglowski 6; oliveromg 5; ultimathule 21; Matka Wariatka 23; Alex Zabusik 14. Superstock: 16; Image Source 12, 19. Every attempt has been made to clear copyright. Should there be any inadvertent omission please apply to the publisher for rectification.